Discovery
E D U C A T I O N ™

Published in 2014 by The Rosen Publishing Group, Inc.
29 East 21st Street, New York, NY 10010

Photo Credits: **KEY** tl=top left; tc=top center; tr=top right; cl=center left; c=center; cr=center right; bl=bottom left; bc=bottom center; br=bottom right; bg=background

CBT = Corbis; DT = Dreamstime; GI = Getty Images; iS = istockphoto.com; PIC = The Picture Desk; SH = Shutterstock; SPL = Science Photo Library; TF = Topfoto; TPL = photolibrary.com; wiki = Wikipedia

1c, c iS; **2–3**tc iS; **4–5**cl GI; **6**bl iS; bl, cl SH; **6–7**bg SH; bg iS; tc DT; **7**br GI; br iS; cr TF; **8**bg, bl SH; tl TF; **8–9**bc iS; **9**tc iS; bg SH; **10**tl iS; tl SH; c wiki; **10–11**bc iS **11**cr, tr iS; **12**bc, bg iS; **12–13**bc PIC; **13**bg, tr iS; cr TF; **14**bg iS; bl TF; tr TPL; **15**bg iS; **16–17**bg iS; bc TF; **17**cr SH; **18**cl, cl, tr iS; **18–19**bl iS; **19**bc, bg, cl iS; **20**bg iS; cr wiki; **20–21**tc TF; **21**bg iS; br TF; bc, cl wiki; **22**cr CBT; bg iS; bc TF; **23**cr GI; bg iS; **24**bc GI; tr TPL; **24–25** bg, bg, bg iS; **25**br iS; **26**bg, c iS; bl SPL; cr wiki; **27**br CBT; bg iS; **28**bc iS; **28–29**bg iS; bc TF; **29**cr CBT; bc GI; tc iS; **30**bg iS; **31**bg iS; br wiki; **32**bg iS

All illustrations copyright Weldon Owen Pty Ltd

Weldon Owen Pty Ltd
Managing Director: Kay Scarlett
Creative Director: Sue Burk
Publisher: Helen Bateman
Senior Vice President, International Sales: Stuart Laurence
Vice President Sales North America: Ellen Towell
Administration Manager, International Sales: Kristine Ravn

Library of Congress Cataloging-in-Publication Data

McFadzean, Lesley.
 Creating and cracking codes / by Lesley McFadzean.
   p. cm. — (Discovery education: discoveries and inventions)
 Includes index.
 ISBN 978-1-4777-1329-7 (library binding) — ISBN 978-1-4777-1500-0 (pbk.) —
ISBN 978-1-4777-1501-7 (6-pack)
 1. Cryptography—Juvenile literature. 2. Ciphers—Juvenile literature. I. Title.
 Z103.3.M37 2014
 652'.8—dc23
                          2012043616

Manufactured in the United States of America

CPSIA Compliance Information: Batch #S13PK3: For Further Information contact Rosen Publishing, New York, New York at 1-800-237-9932

Discovery EDUCATION™

CREATING AND CRACKING CODES

LESLEY MCFADZEAN

PowerKiDS press.

New York

Contents

Codes and Ciphers

C odes and ciphers are used to keep the content of messages secret, but they do this in different ways. Codes substitute entire words or phrases with coded words or numbers. The only way to write or to be able to read a coded message is to use a codebook.

Ciphers replace single letters with other letters. To write or read a cipher, you need to know what the rule is for each letter.

PLAINTEXT AND CIPHERTEXT

A cipher uses a fixed rule, called an algorithm, to turn a readable message in plaintext into an unreadable string of letters, or ciphertext. The person writing the message uses the cipher to encrypt the message. The receiver of the message uses the same cipher to decrypt the message.

How to encrypt a message

1 The secret message is written in plaintext.
2 The cipher (moving along three letters in the alphabet) is used to encrypt the message.
3 The unintelligible ciphertext message is sent.

"Meet at the store" in plaintext

"Phhw dw wkh vwruh" in ciphertext

Cipher

How to decrypt a message

1 Look at the letters in the ciphertext.
2 Use the cipher you and the sender know.
3 Unscramble the ciphertext to read the original message in plaintext.

"Phhw dw wkh vwruh" in ciphertext

"Meet at the store" in plaintext

Cipher

ENIGMA

Cryptographer and cryptanalyst
A cryptographer—from the Greek words *kryptos,* meaning secret, and *graphein,* to write—is the person who writes or encrypts a secret message. The cryptanalyst's job is to examine the secret message, crack the code or cipher, and reveal the original text.

Wartime codes and ciphers
In times of war, codes and ciphers are vital. During World War II, the Germans' Enigma cipher, which encrypted messages using randomly scrambled letters, was believed to be unbreakable.

During the Civil War, the Confederate army used simple ciphers, easily cracked by Union cryptanalysts.

Jean-François Champollion (1790–1832)

The Rosetta Stone
The words on the Rosetta Stone were not deliberately written in code when they were carved in 196 BC. At that time, the Egyptians used three different scripts: hieroglyphs, demotic script, and ancient Greek—and the Stone had the same text written in all three. But when the Rosetta Stone was rediscovered in 1799 in Rashid (also known as Rosetta), in Egypt, no one could read all three scripts. In 1822, Jean-François Champollion, who could speak six ancient Middle Eastern languages, deciphered the words—a list of the achievements of the Egyptian pharaoh.

The Rosetta Stone

Secret messages
Messages can be passed in secret. But if a message falls into the wrong hands, it will no longer be secret. The solution is to use a cipher that only the sender and the receiver know. Then the secret remains safe.

Early Writing

Writing is a way of encoding a message using symbols. Four main systems of writing developed in various parts of the ancient world. The earliest pictographs were small images that denoted common objects or ideas. Cuneiform writing originally used pictographs, but later, symbols, to represent syllables in spoken language. Hieroglyphs used symbols for a sound, syllable, or object. Alphabets are the system of phonetic writing that most Americans and Europeans use today.

Sumerian cuneiform
The Sumerians were the first to develop a writing system, in about 3400 BC. A wedge-shaped stylus, made from a sharpened reed, was used to inscribe the symbols on wet clay tablets. This type of writing system is called cuneiform, from the Latin *cuneus*, meaning wedge.

Hieroglyphs were arranged in neat rows and columns. They could be read left to right, right to left, or up and down.

Ancient Greek
The Greeks were the first Europeans to develop a writing system based on an alphabet. Eventually, the Ionian alphabet of 25 letters was adopted and all other European alphabets developed from it.

Egyptian hieroglyphs

There were 700 Egyptian hieroglyphs. Some of these stood for entire words, but most hieroglyphs stood for individual sounds, or for groups of sounds or syllables. That is, hieroglyphs were a form of phonetic writing.

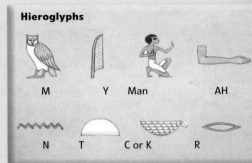

Hieroglyphs

M	Y	Man	AH

N	T	C or K	R

Phaistos disk

This clay disk was discovered in 1908 in a Minoan palace at Phaistos, in Greece. It probably dates back to 1850 BC. On both sides of the disk, there are more than 240 pictographs, which nobody has been able to decipher.

Scribes in training

For ancient Egyptian boys, it was an honor to be trained from a young age to become a scribe.

HILZINSPDFUVEOBDGRFMUECKNSAYSTGP

THE SCYTALE

The first encryption device was used by the Spartans from 400 BC. Both the sender and the receiver had a baton, called a scytale, of equal diameter. The message, written on a long strip of leather, was a jumble of scrambled letters when it was not wrapped around the scytale.

Spartan battles
The scytale was used for carrying messages to and from battlefields.

Decryption
The receiver wrapped the strip around his baton to line up the letters in the message.

Encryption
A message was written on a strip of leather around a baton. Then the strip was taken off.

First Military Ciphers

The oldest means of keeping a written message secret is steganography—concealing the message so no one knows that it exists. Demaratus, a Spartan living in Persia, sent what looked like an unused wax writing tablet to Sparta, Greece, in 480 BC, to warn of a Persian attack. He had written directly on the wood then covered the message with a new layer of wax.

Eighty years later, the Spartans developed the world's first encryption device, known as a scytale, and since that time, codes, ciphers, and steganography have been used to communicate military and political secrets.

The full name of the world's first known cryptanalyst was Abu Yusuf Yaqub ibn Ishaq al-Sabbah Al-Kindi.

Al-Kindi

Al-Kindi (c. AD 800–873), a scholar in Baghdad, pointed out the main problem with simple ciphers. The number of letters and their frequency in the plaintext remains the same in the ciphertext, which makes it easier to crack the cipher.

The Caesar cipher

Julius Caesar used a very basic cipher that shifted letters three places along the alphabet so that "C " became "F." Any displacement or substitution cipher such as this became known as a Caesar cipher.

| A | B | C | D | E | F | G | H | I | J | K | L | M | N | O | P | Q | R | S | T | U | V | W | X | Y | Z |

| A | B | C | D | E | F | G | H | I | J | K | L | M | N | O | P | Q | R | S | T | U | V | W | X | Y | Z |

Gaius Julius Caesar

Julius Caesar (100–44 BC) knew that military conquests brought power. Over a 13-year period, he fought and won 10 battles out of 12 and, during this time, his messages were encrypted using a cipher. But compared with the Spartan's scytale, invented 342 years earlier, the Caesar cipher was easy to crack.

Polyalphabetic cipher encryption

In a polyalphabetic cipher (*poly* means many), the letters in the encrypted message use many different algorithms. To remember what these different algorithms are, a code word is selected. The number of places away from A in the alphabet of each of the letters in the code word then become the algorithms.

A	B	C	D	E	F	G	H	I	J	K	L	M	N	O	P	Q	R	S	T	U	V	W	X	Y	Z
	1	2	3	4	5	6	7	8	9	10	11	12	13	14	15	16	17	18	19	20	21	22	23	24	25

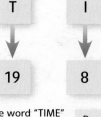

T	I	M	E
19	8	12	4

A code word (for example, "TIME") is used to encrypt the plaintext. Each letter in the plaintext is shifted a different number of places away from A in the alphabet.

Here, the code word "TIME" and the number of places away from A of each of its four letters (that is, 19, 8, 12, 4) is used. By repeating this number sequence, the plaintext "HIDE GUNS IN FOREST" becomes the ciphertext "AQPI ZCZW BV RSKMEX." How "HIDE" is encrypted as "AQPI" is shown here.

PLAINTEXT LETTER	KEY LETTER	POSITIONS TO SHIFT PLAINTEXT	CIPHERTEXT LETTER
H	T	19	A
I	I	8	Q
D	M	12	P
E	E	4	I

Key letter: T means shift 19 positions

H	I	J	K	L	M	N	O	P	Q	R	S	T	U	V	W	X	Y	Z	A
	1	2	3	4	5	6	7	8	9	10	11	12	13	14	15	16	17	18	19

Key letter: I means shift 8 positions

I	J	K	L	M	N	O	P	Q
	1	2	3	4	5	6	7	8

Key letter: M means shift 12 positions

D	E	F	G	H	I	J	K	L	M	N	O	P
	1	2	3	4	5	6	7	8	9	10	11	12

Key letter: E means shift 4 positions

E	F	G	H	I
	1	2	3	4

Polyalphabetic Ciphers

aesar ciphers were much too easy to decrypt. If a cryptanalyst could work out the rule or algorithm for one letter, the same algorithm applied to all the other letters and the message could be deciphered. Polyalphabetic ciphers are more complex because each plaintext letter follows a different algorithm to create the ciphertext letter. There is a double-locking system on polyalphabetic ciphers that makes the cryptanalyst's task much more difficult.

A QUEEN'S DOWNFALL

Mary, Queen of Scots, was imprisoned in the Tower of London by Queen Elizabeth I of England. Mary sent and received encrypted letters from her supporters. Symbols were used for individual letters (cipher) but also for words (code). Thomas Phelippes, one of the best cryptanalysts in Europe, read all Mary's letters, including one about a planned revolt against Queen Elizabeth I. Mary was executed.

Mary, Queen of Scots

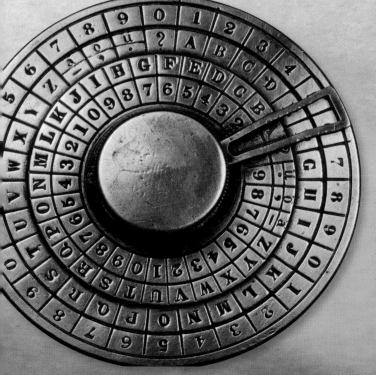

Alberti cipher disk
During the Civil War, the Union army used this disk to encrypt and decrypt messages. By moving the arm around the disk, ciphertext letters and numbers could be converted into plaintext letters and numbers.

Grilles

n 1550, a completely new cryptographic tool was invented by Girolamo Cardano. The Cardano grille combined two systems: steganography (a concealed message that is embedded or hidden from sight) and ciphers. The grille was a physical mask, like a paper stencil, with cut-out holes. When laid over an innocent message, the holes revealed the letters of the concealed message.

Just as Caesar ciphers were improved over time, so were grilles. But it took 330 years for the turning grille to be invented.

Sending the message
For the first few months of World War I, the German army used a turning grille to encrypt messages. These were then telegraphed using Morse code.

The Cardano grille

To encrypt or decipher, both sender and receiver must have the key—a grille with holes in identical positions. The grille holes reveal only the letters in the secret message.

Encryption
The message must seem totally innocent but it should not be too clumsy or stilted. The only letters that matter are those revealed by the grille holes.

I will be at the opera tonight, but will meet you for dinner later, if you like.

*I will **b**e at the **o**pera tonight, but **w**ill meet you for dinner l**a**te**r**, if you lik**e***

Girolamo Cardano
Girolamo Cardano (1501–1576) was an Italian inventor and mathematician. Like many people, he was fascinated by secret messages.

Decryption
The grille is placed over the top to reveal the message. Although it was easy to use a grille, it was also easy for the grille to be lost, stolen, or sold.

Fernsprecher

The turning grille

This grille was divided into four quadrants with four holes in each quadrant. The grille was not laid only once over the original message. It was turned in a number of directions and laid over the message after each turn to eventually reveal the secret letters.

1 The first 16 letters

Using the same plaintext message as page 14, the first 16 secret letters, four in each of the four quadrants, are written using the grille holes.

2 First turn

The sender turns the grille 90 degrees counterclockwise, then writes the next 16 letters, four in each quadrant.

3 Second turn

By turning the grille a further 90 degrees counterclockwise, letters 33–48 are written.

4 Final turn

Turning another 90 degrees for the last time, the remaining secret letters and filler letters (called nulls), which make a total of 64 letters, are written.

5 Ciphertext message

The message of 64 letters, 16 per quadrant, is unreadable without the turning grille and without knowing the turns required.

Newspaper Code

From the eighteenth century, secret messages could be passed from one person to another in newspapers. These secret messages often appeared in personal columns, placed by lovers, spies, and even criminals.

Before electronic communication, news reporters had to read out—or shout—their news reports on a public telephone, or they had to send a telegram from the post office. Another reporter could hear or read the report. By using code words, reporters could get a scoop without their fellow reporters knowing the real message.

Everest conquered
The news that Edmund Hillary and Tenzing Norgay had climbed to the summit of Mount Everest was a scoop for James Morris, a journalist with the *Times* in London, England, who was traveling with them. Using a few agreed code words related to the Everest climb, Morris sent a message that suggested the attempt had been abandoned when, in fact, his coded report said that Everest had been conquered and gave the names of the two conquerors.

Tenzing Norgay
Tenzing Norgay almost succeeded in climbing Everest in 1952. In 1953, he did succeed.

CRYPTIC CLUES

From the 1920s, many newspapers printed crosswords with cryptic (enigmatic or secret) clues. Cryptanalysis is used to solve the clues. The clues can be ciphers, such as an anagram, which has rearranged letters. Clues can also be in code, where a word is replaced with another word.

Cryptic crossword

Edmund Hillary
There were several climbers in the expedition, but Hillary reached the summit.

" Snow conditions bad. Advanced base abandoned. Awaiting improvement. "

Coded message	Meaning
Snow conditions bad	Everest climbed
Wind still troublesome	Attempt abandoned
South Col untenable	Band
Lhotse Face impossible	Bourdillon
Ridge camp untenable	Evans
Withdrawal to West Basin	Gregory
Advanced base abandoned	Hillary
Camp 5 abandoned	Hunt
Camp 6 abandoned	Lowe
Camp 7 abandoned	Noyce
Awaiting improvement	Tenzing
Further news follows	Ward

Morse Code

Millions of people around the world know Morse code. It is not a secret code but a way of sending or transmitting messages. It was invented in 1835 by American Samuel Morse, and used a combination of dots and dashes for each of the letters of the alphabet, numbers, and punctuation. The coded message of dots and dashes was then transmitted by electrical impulses down a wire, in a system called telegraphy.

Morse code was the first form of instant messaging. It was abandoned as an official message system in 2008.

Samuel Finley Breese Morse

SAMUEL MORSE

Samuel Morse was a professor of Arts and Design at New York University when he came up with the idea for Morse code. However, he and his partners struggled for many years to get funding for the new telegraphy system. It was not until 1844 that the first Morse code message was transmitted—from the Capitol, in Washington, D.C., to Baltimore.

Sending messages
A simple machine transmitted the dots and dashes by sending electrical impulses down a wire. The sender pressed down the key briefly for a dot, and three times longer for a dash.

1920s telegraph

Other transmission methods
As well as telegraphy, there are other ways to transmit Morse code messages. A foghorn or a flashlight can either sound or flash the dots and dashes that make up the message.

The Morse alphabet

There are two Morse code alphabets. The International Morse code, shown here, is used in most parts of the world except the United States. Some of the most commonly used letters—such as E, T, and S—have short codes that are easy to remember. The US Morse code alphabet—Morse's original code—shares the same symbols as the International alphabet for 15 of the 26 letters, but has a different combination of dots and dashes for 11 letters.

INTERNATIONAL MORSE CODE

A	•—	N	—•
B	—•••	O	———
C	—•—•	P	•——•
D	—••	Q	——•—
E	•	R	•—•
F	••—•	S	•••
G	——•	T	—
H	••••	U	••—
I	••	V	•••—
J	•———	W	•——
K	—•—	X	—••—
L	•—••	Y	—•——
M	——	Z	——••

Using the key
The operator presses down on the knob, holding it for a short time for a dot and a longer time for a dash.

Remembering the code
Morse code is not an easy code to memorize. The alphabet shown here, with the dots and dashes of International Morse code superimposed on the letters, was used by soldiers in World War I.

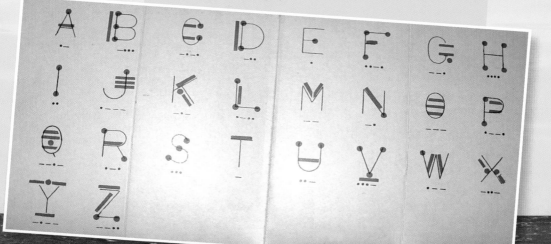

U-boat attacks to resume

After a U-boat sank the ocean liner the *Lusitania* in 1915, killing US civilians, Germany promised that it would stop attacks on neutral ships. The telegram revealed that the Germans were about to restart unrestricted U-boat attacks.

Coded telegram
The telegram was encrypted in numeric code from the latest German codebook.

The Zimmerman Telegram

World War I broke out in 1914. The United States remained neutral until, in 1917, the British gave the Americans a decoded German telegram sent by the German Foreign Minister, Arthur Zimmerman, to Mexico. It revealed that German U-boat attacks on shipping in the Atlantic Ocean would resume, and Mexico was "offered" Texas, Arizona, and New Mexico if it became a German ally.

The cryptanalysts
Captain Reginald Hall led a team of cryptanalysts in Room 40, the British military decoding center. The British had captured German codebooks early in the war, which gave them some clues. But they did not have the right codebook, so some guesswork was required to decode the telegram.

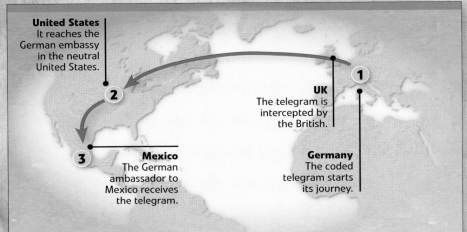

United States
It reaches the German embassy in the neutral United States.

2

1

UK
The telegram is intercepted by the British.

3

Mexico
The German ambassador to Mexico receives the telegram.

Germany
The coded telegram starts its journey.

TELEGRAM ROUTE

The British had cut all of Germany's transatlantic cables, so the telegram was sent through normal telegraph lines from Germany to the United States, then Mexico. The British were monitoring messages to and from Germany on the unsecured telegraph lines and intercepted the telegram.

1 Confident the telegram could not be decoded, Zimmerman sent it on January 19, 1917.

2 The telegram (being decoded by the British) was routed via the German embassy in Washington, D.C.

3 The telegram for the Mexican president reached Mexico.

Decoding
Cryptanalysts used captured codebooks and some lateral thinking to decode the telegram.

The message
The decoded message was given to the US president on February 24, 1917.

US declares war
News of the Zimmerman telegram was published in the United States. Then, on April 6, 1917, President Woodrow Wilson declared war.

Enigma Cipher

The Enigma cipher machine was patented in 1918 by a German businessman, Arthur Scherbius. It was originally used by banks and businesses to encode communications for security reasons. From 1924, it was adapted by the German military. Additional scramblers were added and their positions were changed every day.

The Germans were sure they had an unbreakable cipher, and by the end of the war they had more than 30,000 Enigma machines operating. The machines were portable and could be used on the battlefield, in the air, or in a U-boat. Operators set up the machine using that day's codes for scrambler positions, then they typed in the plaintext and the machine did all the encryption.

That's Amazing!

After every plaintext letter was typed, the three rotors changed position. The next time that plaintext letter was typed, it was encrypted differently. So the cipher was much harder to crack.

Bletchley Park
The British Government Code and Cipher School was set up at Bletchley Park in August 1939. The team had experienced mathematicians, code breakers, linguists, and historians.

The rotors
The Enigma machine used three rotors, also known as scrambler disks. The position of each rotor was changed daily.

The Enigma machine

There were billions of possible permutations on the Enigma machine. The day code determined: which three of the machine's five rotors were used; the position of the three selected rotors; the starting position or letter for each rotor; and the wiring of the plugboard. Different day codes were used by the German army, air force, and navy.

Reflector
The reflector sent each letter back through the rotors to be rescrambled.

Rotor
Each letter was scrambled as it passed through the three rotors.

Lampboard
After scrambling, the ciphertext letter came up in the lampboard.

Plugboard
The plugboard was another scrambler, rewired every day.

Cracking Enigma

Alan Turing
Alan Turing, a cryptanalyst at Bletchley Park, specialized in binary mathematics. He developed the "bombe," also called the Turing machine, which replicated, or copied, the settings of the Enigma machine.

S everal things played a role in cracking the Enigma cipher. As well as having early Polish-built Enigma machines, mathematical analysis by the world's first computer, and captured Enigma codebooks, the British had a team of brilliant cryptanalysts. The Germans believed the Enigma cipher was unbreakable and they never knew that a team at Bletchley Park decrypted Enigma communications throughout the war.

The code name for the interception and decryption of Enigma communications was Ultra. It was one of the most successful intelligence operations in history, and it remained secret until the 1990s.

Colossus
The world's first electronic digital information processor, Colossus, used vacuum tubes to analyze the huge amount of mathematical data required to crack codes. This version, the Colossus Mark 2, used 2,400 vacuum tubes to help crack the Enigma cipher.

Code breakers' dilemma
After cracking the Enigma cipher, the British had to be very careful how they used the decoded information. If they acted on a decoded message, for example by evacuating an identified air-raid target, the Germans would know Enigma was no longer secure and would change to a new cipher system.

CRACKING THE CODE

Cracking the Enigma cipher involved Polish cryptanalysts, Polish-built Enigma machines, and the French Secret Service as well as the British linguists and mathematicians at Bletchley Park.

1 A Polish cryptanalyst discovered that many Enigma messages started with the same words *Aus aus*. From these repeated letters he found links to decipher other letters.

2 The French Deuxième Bureau handled a German spy who provided them with some details of the military Enigma machine and day codes.

3 The British used this information to build their own Enigma machine and calculators, or bombes, to work out the possible permutations of letters in the Enigma cipher.

A → U
B   M
C   X
D   N
E   C
F   B
G   V
H   Q
I   P
J   W
K   O
L   E
M   I
N   R
O   Z
P   T
Q   Y
R   L
S → A
T   K
U → S
V   J
W   D
X   H
Y   F
Z   G

Unbreakable cryptosystem

A one-time pad is an unbreakable cryptosystem only if it is used 100 percent correctly. Every cipher key must be used only once. However, after coming up with the random data needed for a key, it is tempting to reuse the key—Soviet spies did this for a short period in the 1940s. Also, only two people can have a copy of the key. When MI5, the British intelligence agency, captured a one-time pad from a Soviet spy, the cipher key for that message was no longer unbreakable.

Joseph Oswald Mauborgne
Captain Joseph Mauborgne of the US Army Signal Corps suggested to his co-inventor, Gilbert Vernam, that the key for the one-time pad should contain random information. Their idea was patented in the mid-1920s.

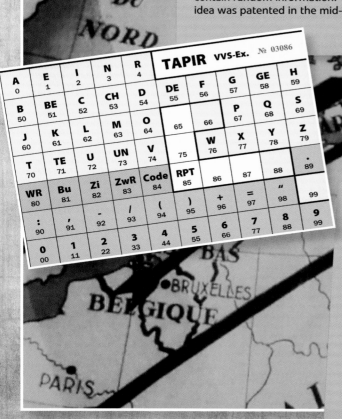

A 0	E 1	I 2	N 3	R 4	**TAPIR** VVS-Ex. № 03086			
					DE 55	F 56	G 57	GE 58	H 59
B 50	BE 51	C 52	CH 53	D 54			P 67	Q 68	S 69
J 60	K 61	L 62	M 63	O 64	65	66	W 76	X 77	Y 78	Z 79
T 70	TE 71	U 72	UN 73	V 74	75				
WR 80	Bu 81	Zi 82	ZwR 83	Code 84	RPT 85	86	87	88	. 89
: 90	' 91	- 92	/ 93	(94	) 95	+ 96	= 97	" 98	99
0 00	1 11	2 22	3 33	4 44	5 55	6 66	7 77	8 88	9 99

The four rules for one-time pad

1 The cipher key must contain totally random data. Because it is random, clues (such as the frequency of use of certain letters) are eradicated.

2 Only two people have the key—the sender who encrypts the message and the receiver who decrypts it.

3 The key of random data must be the same length as the plaintext message.

4 Each key can be used only once and must be destroyed after this single use. After a message has been encrypted, the key used to encrypt it must never be used again.

The One-Time Pad

The one-time pad, also known as the Vernam cipher, was invented by Gilbert Vernam, an engineer at the American Telephone & Telegraph Company, and US army Captain Joseph Mauborgne. The co-inventors were American, but one-time pads were widely used by spies from the Soviet Union, which was the enemy of the United States during the Cold War.

The one-time pad is complicated and time-consuming to use, but is the only encryption technique that cannot be broken—theoretically. It is small enough to fit in the palm of one hand. For these reasons, it was used by spies right up until the 1980s, 60 years after it was invented.

That's Amazing!

The encryption system of the one-time pad is still in use today—as the stream cipher used by modern Web browsers to encrypt messages exchanged with security-protected Web sites.

THE VENONA PROJECT

From the early 1940s until 1980, during the Cold War, the US and British governments worked together on the Venona Project. This monitored government and intelligence communications in and out of the Soviet Union. Many of the coded messages were encrypted using one-time pads.

The Rosenbergs
The US citizens Julius and Ethel Rosenberg were two of the many Soviet spies unmasked by the Venona Project. They were found guilty of passing US atomic secrets to the Soviet Union and were both executed in 1953.

Fact File

Cryptography (writing messages in code or cipher) and steganography (hiding messages in transit) are both intended to conceal and confuse. Many techniques are used in steganography, from swallowing messages to hiding them in microdots or using invisible ink.

You do not have to be a code breaker to use some of these techniques, which have been adapted and are used in everyday life.

Mazes and labyrinths

Mazes and many labyrinths are designed to conceal the correct route and to confuse anyone who enters. The most famous labyrinth is in the Greek myth of Theseus and the Minotaur. As Theseus found his way to the center of the labyrinth to slay the Minotaur, he unrolled a ball of thread, or clew, which we now spell "clue."

The [girl] put on a [coat] and [boots] to play in the [rain].

Rebus

A rebus replaces words or syllables with pictures. It is a form of substitution code. The early Christians used rebuses to encode their messages to each other. They are used in heraldry, where the name of the bearer is pictorial. Today, rebuses are used to teach children to read.

This sentence is "The girl put on a coat and boots to play in the rain."

Secrets on silk

Silk is soft but durable and can be folded up to be very small. In ancient China, messengers would roll silk containing a written secret message into a tight ball, cover it in wax, and swallow it. Pilots in World War II hid small maps, written on silk, in case they were shot down.

Cipher key on silk

Braille

Braille, invented by the blind teenager Louis Braille in the nineteenth century, is based on Charles Barbier's code. Raised dots and dashes let French soldiers read and write messages at night without a light. Louis Braille simplified the code by eliminating the dashes and halving the number of dots. Braille is read by passing the fingertips over the dots.

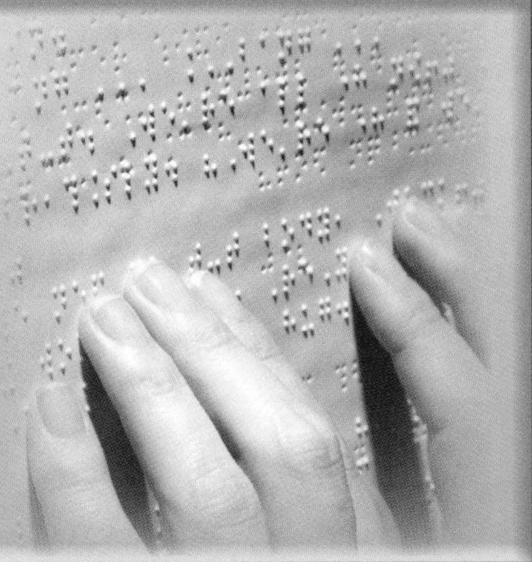

Reading braille

Invisible ink

The writer Pliny the Elder used invisible ink in ancient Rome. More recently, an al-Qaeda contact list was found written in invisible ink. Simple invisible inks are made from lemon juice, wine, vinegar, or milk. Prisoners of war used sweat, saliva, and urine. Ultraviolet light, heat, or chemicals are needed to reveal the invisible message.

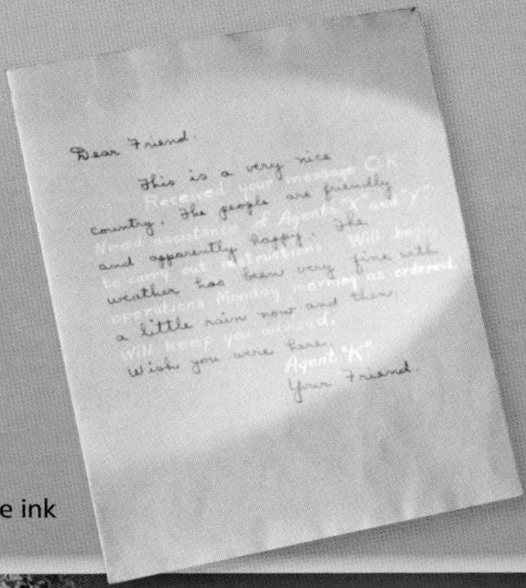

Message in invisible ink

Microdots

A microdot is text shrunk to the size and shape of a period. This is a form of steganography because it is not immediately visible on the printed page. The microdot shown here led to the spies Peter and Helen Kroger being imprisoned for 20 years.

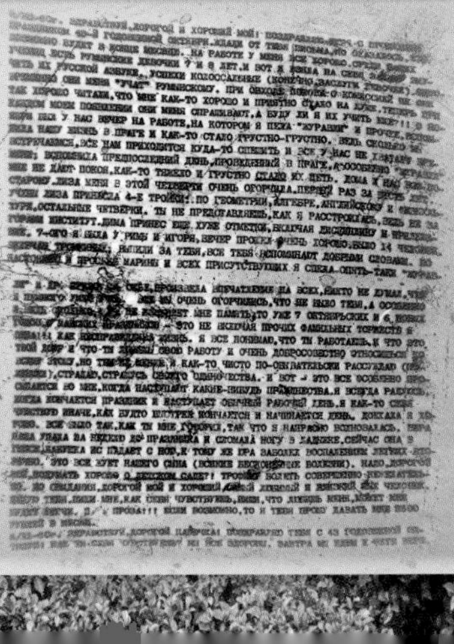

Enlarged microdot showing a page typed by Helen Kroger

Glossary

algorithm
(AL-guh-rih-thum) A step-by-step set of rules that is used, and repeated, to create a secret cipher.

bombe (BOM)
An electromechanical machine with a number of rotating drums that copied the actions of several Enigma machines wired together.

braille (BRAYL) A system of writing that uses raised dots in place of letters so that the writing can be read using the sense of touch.

cipher (SY-fur) A system in which individual letters of plain, readable text are rearranged or replaced with other letters according to a secret rule.

ciphertext (SY-fur-tekst)
The unreadable string of letters that results when letters of readable text have been changed or substituted using a secret cipher.

code (COHD) A system that replaces words or phrases with other words, groups of letters, or numbers so that the message cannot be read by anyone without the codebook.

cryptanalyst
(kript-A-nuh-list) A code breaker; a person who tries to decipher encrypted messages and change them back into readable words without knowing the key or algorithm for unlocking the cipher or code.

cryptic (KRIHP-tik)
Describes something that is secret or mysterious.

cryptographer
(krip-TAH-gruh-fur) A code writer; a person who writes a message in code or cipher.

cryptography
(krip-TAH-gruh-fee) The art of writing, and of solving, secret codes and ciphers.

cuneiform
(kyu-NEE-uh-form) A form of writing in wedge-shaped characters, usually on clay; used by ancient Babylonians.

decipher (dih-SY-fur)
To convert an unreadable message, written in cipher, back into the original plain, readable text by cracking or unlocking the cipher system.

decode
(dee-COHD) To convert an unreadable message, written in code, back into the original plain, readable text by cracking the code used.

decrypt (dee-KRIPT)
To convert an unreadable, secret message back into plain, readable language by deciphering or decoding it.

encipher (en-SY-fur)
To use a cipher system to turn a readable message into an unreadable string of letters.

Enigma cipher
(ih-NIHG-muh SY-fur)
A cipher created by the special Enigma encrypting machine that was used by the Germans during World War II.

grille (GRIHL) A piece of paper or card, with several holes cut in it, which is placed over a plaintext message to reveal only certain letters that form a secret message.

hieroglyph (HY-er-uh-glif)
A picture or symbol of an everyday object, which represents a specific sound or consonant. Several hieroglyphs together form a word.

microdot (MY-kroh-dot)
A photograph of a document, taken with a special camera that reduces the text to the size of a typewritten period. A microdot is usually hidden on a page of normal text.

Morse code
(MORS KOHD) A telegraph code, invented by Samuel Morse, that uses short dots and longer dashes to represent the letters of the alphabet.

null (NUHL) A dummy letter, symbol, or number inserted into an encrypted message to make up the required number of letters or to make the message more difficult to decrypt.

numeric code
(noo-MEHR-ik COHD) A code that uses numbers in place of words or phrases.

one–time pad
(WUN-tym PAD) A small pad or notebook that contains the key to an encrypted message; the key is used once only then destroyed.

phonetic (fun-NEH-tik)
Describes a form of writing where symbols, such as letters, correspond to sounds.

pictograph (PIK-toh-graf)
A symbol or small picture used to represent a word or phrase; also called a pictogram.

plaintext (PLAYN-tekst)
A message using normal letters and words, which can be easily read before it is encrypted.

random (RAN-dum)
Describes a process by which an end result (such as the algorithms for a cipher) is determined without any definite method or rule; something done in a haphazard way or solely by chance.

rebus (REE-bus) The use of pictures, symbols, or objects to represent words or the sounds of words.

scrambler (SKRAM-blur)
A device that jumbles or muddles the letters in a message so that they cannot be read by anyone who does not have the descrambling device.

scytale (SKIH-tuh-lee)
A wooden rod or baton with a strip of leather wrapped around it, on which a secret message is written.

steganography
(steh-guh-NAW-gruh-fee)
From the Greek *steganos* (covered) and *graphy* (writing), steganography is the art of hiding a secret message in an ordinary, plaintext message so that no one suspects that a secret message exists.

telegraphy
(the-LEH-gruh-fee)
The sending or transmitting of messages over long distances by making and breaking electrical connections.

Index

Websites

Due to the changing nature of Internet links, PowerKids Press has developed an online list of websites related to the subject of this book. This site is updated regularly. Please use this link to access the list:
www.powerkidslinks.com/disc/code/